Silver Linings

Sisters

Stories to Warm Your Heart

new seasons
™

a division of Publications International, Ltd.

Contributing writers: Gail Cohen, Christine A. Dallman, Luci N. Fuller, Margaret Anne Huffman, Marie D. Jones, Karen M. Leet, Ann Russell, Donna Shryer, Diana L. Thrift, Natalie Walker Whitlock

Front cover: Fine Art Photographic Library, London/Art Resource

Louis Weber, CEO
Publications International, Ltd.
7373 North Cicero Avenue
Lincolnwood, Illinois 60712

Manufactured in China.

8 7 6 5 4 3 2 1

ISBN: 0-7853-4240-0

Library of Congress Card Number: 00-110304

What does it mean to have a loving sister?

It means that someone who

understands our past will walk

with us into the future.

Contents

A Friend for Life

The only child believes that she isn't missing anything by not having sisters. It's just as well that she never will know better.

*T*he relationship between sisters is as strong as any bond there is. Your sister has been there since the beginning: She knows you almost as well as you know yourself. And when you forget who you are, you can always count on her to remind you.

As anyone lucky enough to have a sister knows, making time for your sister is as important as making time for yourself—in fact, it's almost the same thing. Your sister is someone who knows your true shoe size, dress size, and hair color, but, most important, she knows the things that touch your heart. And you know you can always count on each other, especially when it comes time to count your blessings.

Throughout life's journey, as young girls grow into mature women, one thing remains the same. As sisters grow up and grow older, forging lives of their own—separate from the life they shared as children—they do not grow apart. The bond is too deep, too unshakable to break, held together by years of shared laughter, tears, and adventures. The sister who rescued you when you fell on the playground will become the woman who holds your hand when your grown-up life is hard. And, whether the times you remember are filled with support and laughter or squabbles and tiffs (and your memories are sure to include plenty of both), one thing is certain: The relationship you've built is one to treasure.

Sisters come in perfectly matched sets and in intriguing assortments. The heartwarming stories in this book prove that whether older sister or younger, twin sister or stepsister, sister-in-law or adoptive sister, one thing remains the same: A sister is a friend for life—someone to laugh with, learn from, and love.

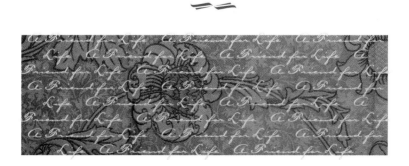

Growing Together

Many sisters know one another well and are close from the beginning. But sometimes the journey of discovering a sister's friendship happens over time.

Other than the infamous roaster incident, Sandy and Kathy had a fairly quiet relationship as sisters. Of course, as victim of the long-ago roasting pan incident, Kathy still vividly recalls the dent her head made in the large, white-speckled pan when Sandy brought their argument to an abrupt halt with one swift blow. Kathy claims to have seen stars. Sandy still denies that any dent was made in the roaster. Posterity will never be able to put together the clues: Was it Miss Sandy, in the kitchen, with the roaster? Alas, the trail is too cold now.

Today, however—forty-some years after this roaster made its way into family lore—Sandy and Kathy enjoy the close bonds of sisterhood. These bonds were not always as they are now. Like the opening of a flower, the beauty of their relationship unfolded over time.

They are several years apart in age; consequently, they did not experience the bonding that often happens between sisters with only one, two, or even three years separating them. The girls grew up with a certain distance between them, too far removed in years to relate to each other's worlds.

As adults, they lived within half an hour's drive of each other, but their social circles continued to be separate. They were in contact and occasionally visited or shopped with their young children in tow, enjoying the time together and catching up on each other's lives, but their divergent lifestyles did little to promote a depth of friendship or closeness between them.

Time has a funny way of changing things. Nests were emptying as their children began spreading fledgling wings. With this imminent dispersion, family get-togethers became more significant to the sisters. The few threads of relationship that had held them together grew stronger.

Then their father died. The sisters provided their mother with the support she needed, and as a team, they arranged for their father's funeral. There was deep pain, but they did not feel it separately. There was no chasm to reach across. They were standing near enough to touch, near enough to comfort, near enough to understand what sisters are meant to be. Together they grieved.

Sandy and Kathy have held onto what they found in the years between their childhood and their father's passing. Many sisters know one another well and are close from the beginning. But sometimes the journey of discovering a sister's friendship happens over time. So it has been with Kathy and Sandy. And so their journey will continue.

A sister is a forever friend.

—AMERICAN PROVERB

My Sister Was an Only Child

I met my sisters when I was five, but I don't recall the first time I saw them. Mara, the oldest, said I was a scrawny thing, all skin and bones, with huge frightened eyes, and clutching a shabby teddy. I was pretty much an orphan; my mother had died during childbirth, and Daddy couldn't raise me alone. So Mama took me in along with her other two, Mara, who'd been left on the church steps, and Rosie, as Irish as you could get, with frizzy red hair, freckles, and fair skin. Rosie had family—too much of it, actually. They had run out of space, food, and strength by the time she came along, so Mama took her in, too.

They were both much older than me. Mara told me they weren't all that pleased to see me: another mouth to feed, more feet to keep in shoes. Things were tight enough already, with Mama trying to feed most of the neighborhood when they went hungry. Mama could stretch a soupbone to feed 20 if she could find enough potatoes and carrots.

Mara said she and Rosie tormented me every chance they got, which I remember some. She said they got used to me quick enough, and I asked her when they got to liking me. Mara didn't have to think about that at all before she answered.

"Those first weeks you'd whimper in your sleep," Mara told me. "I'd sit on the edge of the bed, singing one of Rosie's Irish songs real soft to shush you so you didn't disturb Mama, since she might have to go out on a call to deliver a baby any time and needed her rest. You were all soft and warm and little."

Rosie thought for a while, then told me, "I started liking you when I painted nail polish on your toenails while we listened to my favorite radio programs."

The two of them took care of me like two busy little moms. They walked me back and forth to school, stopping to tie my shoes every so often. They helped me butter my bread and brush my hair and learn my spelling words. Later, Mara taught me to whip eggs up all light and fluffy for a fine omelette. Rosie guided my fingers on the old piano in the parlor until I could play all our favorite songs by heart.

We quarreled some, like all sisters do. We learned to stick together, though. Rosie cut down outgrown dresses for me, and Mara helped me let down the hems when I started growing fast. They leaned over books with me and listened while I practiced spelling words. They took me to Saturday afternoon double features, filling me up with popcorn, though Mama gave me a nickel if I'd sit between Rosie and Jimmy Jackson whenever we went.

When I started filling out, they teased me, but not in a mean or hateful way at all. They took me shopping with their own money once they had some, and they taught me to sway back and forth on braced feet when we rode the subway car downtown to the department stores. I loved them with my whole heart and wanted nothing better than to grow up as fine and sweet as they both were. I wanted to dress the way they did and walk the way they did and have my hair styled the same way, too.

They always laughed when I imitated them. Mama laughed, too, throwing her head back and hugging us all at the same time, which took some doing, big as we'd all gotten. We weren't any of us related. Not really. But we helped one another. We cared fiercely. We were sisters.

The day I won the spelling bee up on stage in front of the whole school, Mara and Rosie were there watching, clapping harder and longer than anyone else. They walked me home afterward, taking the long way so we could stop off at the park swings, then treated for hot fudge sundaes, my absolute favorite.

I missed them terribly when they left home for jobs and homes of their own, marriages and babies. But they dropped by to visit, bringing their sweet babies for Mama to spoil and always carrying little treats and gifts for me. We'd put our heads together in the kitchen, always our favorite place, and I'd tell them my secrets and ask their advice, which they gladly gave, along with warm hugs and encouragement.

Today, all grown up, married, and with children of my own, I go see them as often as I can. I sing all the old Irish songs to Mara's children, and when Rosie was in the hospital after an emergency appendectomy, I painted her nails for her, which made her smile.

I had been an orphan, on my own, but they had taken me into their hearts and were my sisters. We aren't anything to one another by birth. We aren't related at all. But we are family in our hearts, sisters in our spirits.

She's Still Tall to Me

I was born almost two years after my older sister. So as far as physical stature, I literally had to look up to her during our growing years. But in the end, I managed to shoot past her by two full inches. I can now call her my "little" sister if I want to.

Funny thing, though, I still find myself looking up to her. And it's not because she wears three-inch heels. It's something that reaches beyond growth charts. There is a depth of admiration I carry in my heart for my "big" sister—a feeling that cannot be measured or weighed.

Perhaps my reverence for Tammy began as instinct. I wanted to emulate everything I saw my older, wiser sister doing. I followed her, copied her words and actions, and fairly drove her to distraction

17

many times. I recall standing at the door with my mother as my sister's ride to kindergarten waited in the driveway. Each morning, I begged for a hug and kiss from her as she left. Only at Mom's urging would Tammy give in to my wish, which slowed her down in her hurry to join her friends. I think the only reason she acquiesced so easily was that she knew I would wail in disappointment if I failed to collect my special good-bye from her.

My little-sister instincts and longing for the security of that familiar older-sister presence created within me a strong confidence in her. When my sister failed math in the second grade, I lived in fear of entering that year of school. I believed with all my heart that if she could not pass that one subject, I would fail altogether!

I sailed through second grade with flying colors and began to realize something. I was a different person than Tammy. It was that very year that, as a fourth grader, Tammy won the local fire department's fire-prevention art contest. A photo of her showed up in our small-town newspaper, and in my mind, my sister was a celebrity.

With the realization that I was more scholarly, athletic, and sensitive, while she was artistic, social, and strong-willed, came the realization that we didn't need to compete with each other. I helped her with homework; she watched out for me at school. Our loyalty to one another ran deep.

When I absentmindedly forgot my lunchbox at home, several blocks away from school, my sister retrieved it for me. She had seen me crying at the lunch table. (My teacher had forbidden me to go get it since I was often forgetful, and this had happened a handful of other times.) When my sister triumphantly returned with my lunch, we both got in trouble. But she confided in me later that if I ever needed her to get it again, she would still come to my rescue, despite the consequences.

My admiration for her grew and grew. Sure, we fought, as sisters do, but she was strong where I was weak, and I appreciated her abilities and admired her tenacity and toughness. She bailed me out in seventh grade when I became the target of a ninth-grade bully's anger. This girl—who was built like a roller-derby champion—began to torment me. When she asked to borrow my felt-marker pens, I didn't dare refuse. She kept them. I said nothing. Then, to my horror, one day I came face to face with her in the hallway. No one else was around, and she grabbed me by the collar of my coat, lifted me off my feet, and shoved me against the wall. I could only stare wide-eyed at her, hoping she would not hit me. Fortunately, some voices from around the corner startled her and she let me drop, assuring me she'd be back.

The mention of her name to my sister brought a frown of recognition. "She's been picking on you?" Tammy asked. "I'll take care of it." My pens were returned the next day, and I even struck up a little rapport with my former nemesis. How my shorter and smaller sister managed to intimidate the school bully, I'll never know. Funny that I didn't ask her. I just thanked her, and we continued on as usual.

So we have continued on into our adult years, my sister in her strength, artistic ability, and compassion, and I in my admiration of her. Tammy has been married for nearly 18 years now, has three handsome boys, works part-time at a medical clinic, and is in the process of getting her nursing degree. I look at her and am proud of everything she is and does.

I often feel her still looking out for me, even across the 500 miles that separate us. Whenever we see each other, I still insist on getting a hug from her. But she doesn't mind anymore. And even though she has to stand on her toes a little to hug me back, in my heart, she's still far taller than I am.

Icing on the Cake

"There! How does it look?" Robin asked. She and Katie examined their joint masterpiece with critical eyes. Rosettes were piped in a perfect circle around the perimeter, and multicolored balloons sailed across a blue frosted sky. Beneath the balloons the words "Happy Birthday, Mom!" were piped in looping calligraphy.

"It's perfect!" Katie pronounced. "I think it's the best cake yet."

"Well, it's certainly better than our first attempt," Robin laughed. "Do you remember that one? What were we, eight, ten years old?"

"The green cake! Our big surprise for Mom...how could I forget?" Katie answered.

The two sisters smiled as they remembered their first, somewhat ill-fated, attempt at baking—an attempt that had spawned a tradition the two carried on to this day.

It was the summer of 1975. Two scrape-kneed, freckle-dusted girls put their pig-tailed heads together, giggling as their mom's Chevy disappeared around the corner. They hauled the Betty Crocker cookbook out of a cabinet, plopping it on the kitchen table with a thud. Scooting back and forth, they collected the ingredients for the cake they planned to bake. Flour, sugar, baking soda (*no soda? we'll substitute extra baking powder*, they determined), salt, butter, eggs (*oops, one rolled off the table and cracked—we'll clean it up later*, they decided), vanilla.... They set busily to work, measuring, sifting, stirring, pouring, baking.

When they pulled it out of the oven, the cake was a little flat and, well, lumpy. Katie peered at it with her head cocked to one side.

"Is this what it's supposed to look like?" she asked dubiously.

Robin, older by two years and far wiser, had the bright idea of leveling the top by cutting off the weird lumps and stuffing them into the valleys. "The frosting will cover it," she insisted.

The sisters had decided ahead of time to frost the cake with green icing, since green was Mom's favorite color. Unfortunately, there was no such thing as green food coloring. So they mixed drops of blue and yellow, but the first try turned out too light—kind of a minty-pistachio color, when Mom's preference leaned more toward a true emerald—so they added more blue (too teal!), and then more yellow (too evergreen!), and so on. The end result was green, all right, and the girls had used up both bottles of food coloring in the process, so the frosting was really, truly, *green*.

They managed to clean up their mess (except for the few drips of dye that had splattered on the table and the floor and refused to be scrubbed off, but Robin thought probably those would fade with time) just before their mother walked in the door. Robin wiped her hands on the back of her legs to get rid of the last of the frosting, and Katie proudly dragged Mom into the kitchen, where the cake sat in the center of the table, resplendent in its lumpy, bumpy, lop-sided, green glory.

Both girls beamed with pride when they carried the cake out after dinner and Mom pronounced it her very favorite birthday cake of all time. It didn't even matter that it tasted like salt and that everyone's lips and teeth looked green in the photos they took to celebrate the occasion.

It was only after the next year's birthday, when the girls attempted a second cake with even less success than they had met the first time, that their mother diplomatically suggested they start helping her in the kitchen more often. After that, Robin and Katie began to get the hang of baking, and a tradition was born. Each year, no matter what was going on, the sisters got together to bake a cake for their mom's birthday and to celebrate their delicious history of sisterhood.

The Worthington Girls

We were known as the Worthington girls growing up. There were four of us. Even though we've all since grown up, married, and moved away, when we're back in town, that's what we're still called. I suppose it's to be expected that one of us would "throw over the traces," as they say around this horse country.

Leave it to Lydia.

The oldest, she's always been a trailblazer, leading us into adventures like the one that once took us on a homemade raft down the river that flowed through our Virginia horse farm. She also set the pace for each of us to graduate from college, find satisfying careers, and establish stable homes. She eventually became a circuit court judge. *Solid*, that's how people described Lydia.

That's how they used to describe her, anyway. Now they call her "that crazy old lady" who gave up a great career and moved to the Colorado boondocks, to a place with no running water, paved roads, or indoor plumbing.

"Do you know what she's doing there?" my youngest sister cried during a conference call. "Building a ranch," she answered her own question, too upset to wait for us to guess. "What on earth does Lydia know about ranching?"

"Does she think she's a cowgirl?" guffawed our witty sister.

"Be serious," I chided. "What is Lydia going to do with a ranch?"

"Lose her money!" the worrier exclaimed. "It's up to us to protect her from herself now that Tommy's not here to do it."

Tommy was Lydia's late husband. I felt uneasy invoking his name since he had always seemed charmed, if bemused, by his wife during their 40 years together and had stood by her no matter how outrageous her antics seemed. And as the years went by, they had become more and more outrageous.

The three of us decided to surprise Lydia with a visit to her "ranch." Hopefully the sight of the Worthington girls would help her come to her senses!

I took time off from my busy dental practice to dovetail with the others' schedules. We planned our "intervention" for Memorial Day weekend and rendezvoused at the St. Louis airport.

"The Worthington girls, together again!" Barbara cried.

We were quiet in our rented car as we drove through foothills that were just coming to life. Wildflowers lined the roads, calves and lambs grazed in lush pastures. My city life seemed washed out, pale, by comparison.

Lydia's driveway, when we finally reached it, was freshly graveled, the entrance marked clearly with hand-hewn timbers.

"Oh, my sisters! The Worthington girls! It's about time you all got here," Lydia cried in delight, without surprise or so much as a protest at our intrusion. "Fences need building, a creek's got to be dammed up before another spring storm takes out the shed I'm using as an infirmary. I'll meet you in the bunkhouse," she continued, pointing to a cabin at the edge of a cleared area. The distant sound of hammering combined with the whine of saws.

Smiling at our open-mouthed astonishment, Lydia pointed to the half-dozen people bustling about the ranch. "Volunteers," she said. "Like you." And with that, she left us standing there in our citified clothes looking as out of place as onions in a petunia patch.

When we tracked Lydia down a little later, she was straddling the ridge pole of a cabin, helping a spotty-faced young man with the roofing. She scrambled down the ladder to see us.

"I expect you're wondering about this place," she said, smiling.

We nodded.

"It's a camp for disadvantaged children," Lydia explained. "Which, sisters dear, we never were."

She saw the bewildered looks on our faces and continued. "Working as a judge, I saw again and again that even the tiniest help a child gets makes a difference in their outcome. I'm creating a place where they can spread their wings, learn to take care of animals," she said, gesturing to high-ground pasture where sheep grazed. "Have you seen the look on a child's face when it rescues an orphaned lamb?"

We shook our heads. "Well, you will," Lydia said firmly. "Camp opens next week."

She was right. We watched the amazing transformation of children realizing their potential, grasping the chance Lydia was offering them and hanging on with all their might. For the first time in their lives, they saw they had a chance. And the Worthington girls were all on hand to see it, too. Three of us were overcome with humility; the fourth had the graciousness not to say "I told you so!"

The night before we left we admired the set of four footprints pressed in the wet concrete foundation of a new cabin the three "sensible" sisters had decided to donate, along with the promise to return with our families to help build it. Those footprints, a permanent, tangible symbol of our commitment to our sister and her cause, were nowhere near as indelible as the lesson we had learned from a "crazy" sister who had made us proud all over again to be called "the Worthington girls."

When sisters are reunited, no matter what their age, girls are together again.

Confidantes and Partners

*W*hen I was 18 months old, I received my favorite gift of all time: my sister. She became my confidante, sensitive to me and my needs, and the perfect partner in crime. As kids, we covered for each other when it came to sneaking an extra snack or staying up late reading under the covers. We shared secrets and advice on everything from boys to clothes to how much we hated coming in earlier than the rest of the kids in the neighborhood. There was nothing we didn't share.

When we were teenagers, we covered for each other about what time we got home from school or a date, we helped each other sneak out of the house, and we went to dances together where we met (and danced with!) older boys. We appreciated knowing we had someone we could trust with our deepest, darkest secrets—and we figured that what our parents didn't know would never hurt them! We had our share of fights and arguments, too. But most of the time we saw the value in sticking together, especially when it came to

29

getting away with things we weren't allowed to do (thanks to loving, but somewhat overprotective parents).

Now we're adults, and we're still confidantes and partners in crime. We continue to cover for each other, share secrets, and complain and give advice about our parents. Sometimes it's over little things—like not wanting our health-conscious mother to know how often we binge on junk food. Or when I'm overextended on my credit cards and want advice, but not a lecture, on money matters. Or when my sister wants to vent her frustration because her teenage kids have a more active social life than she does. But sometimes it's over more serious things, like marriage or health problems, those important secrets that only sisters can share.

There is nothing like a sister when you need someone to just listen—not to try to "fix" you. Being so close in age, with similar values and experiences, my sister and I can help each other in ways that our parents would not understand. They have a different mind-set, want to protect us, and are from a different generation. And being able to cry and scream and whine and complain to someone who will not judge me or baby me—the way a parent might—is a blessing.

I am very close to my husband and share my heart and life with him, but I still find times when I only want to confide in my all-knowing sister. I turn to her when I need to talk about things I trust no one else with. That kind of trust is priceless and rare, even between the best of friends. It's the kind of trust that comes from growing up together.

Today, even with our busy lives, we still find time to be partners in crime—albeit petty crimes such as shopping too much, gossiping about our parents, and overeating. She is more than a sister to me. She is a loyal soul mate on my journey through life.

Your sister knows you almost as well as you know yourself. When you forget who you are, count on her to remind you.

Treasures of Sisterhood

It seemed to Sherri that, in that distant era of childhood, the duration of a single school year had really taken far more time than the quicksilver decades that had somehow passed between her sister's twentieth birthday and the milestone she would be celebrating in just a few days. Time, mused Sherri as she looked up at the calendar that hung on the wall across the room, is a strange thing. There was no doubt that it was rendering her and her sister older, but Sherri also thought of the opportunity that all these years of time had afforded them to build and maintain their relationship. *A treasure*, Sherri mused. *Time has given us the treasure of sisterhood.*

She had been wondering what to give Marilyn on this special birthday, and now with those thoughts, a plan began to form. Somewhere in her basement, an old trunk lay in a dark corner, its clown-design paper fading and peeling, and its belly empty, long retired from years of faithful duty as their toy chest. With some effort, Sherri freed the old trunk from various paraphernalia stored on and around it, and took it upstairs.

After a bit of cleaning and repair work, the chest had just the nostalgic charm for which Sherri had hoped. *Now to fill it,* she smiled to herself in anticipation. Ideas tumbled over one another, but the first item she decided to place in the "treasure box" was something her mother had given to Sherri when she had moved into her first apartment after getting her first job.

"You and your sister used to share this blanket," her mother had told her. "And the two of you would fall asleep under it, holding hands. It was your security to have this blanket and to have each other. I thought you might like to have it as a keepsake." Sherri now lined the old trunk with this relic from their earliest years together.

Next she went to her library—a room lined with bookshelves filled with nearly every book she'd ever owned. She rarely parted with a text once it fell into her possession. But there was one she wanted to give to Marilyn now. An old primer. Marilyn had patiently sat with Sherri at their old kitchen table, teaching her to sound out words from this book. Through all their years of school, Marilyn never seemed to tire of tutoring her younger sister, who would not cooperate with anyone else who tried to help her with her schoolwork.

Sherri spent the next few days filling up the toy box. She purposely burnt a batch of muffins, which she shellacked and placed back in the muffin tin—a reminder of their first attempts at baking together.

In an old scrapbook, Sherri discovered ancient ticket stubs to the movie she and Marilyn and their boyfriends had gone to on their first double date. There was a small, ugly painting on velvet that Marilyn had talked Sherri into buying on a trip they had taken together to Mexico one winter. Sherri remembered that after the purchase, Marilyn had laughed at her. *Marilyn could always talk me into anything,* Sherri shook her head, groaning out loud.

It wasn't long before Sherri had to decide which items would have to be excluded from her collection of memorabilia. *I guess it won't all fit in here,* she admitted to herself. But after much packing and repacking, the gift was finally complete—just the way she wanted it. There was only one thing left to do.

As Sherri sat at her desk to begin a letter of explanation to Marilyn, she smiled and wondered if any such introduction was really necessary. *Marilyn will just know,* Sherri thought. She thought of Marilyn's smile and the fun they would have rummaging through the toy box. Yes, theirs was a long and happy history. Time had been their friend and had given them the treasure of friendship.

"May there be many more treasures ahead for us," Sherri wrote simply. "Happy birthday, Big Sister."

My Real Sister

My friend Amy was admiring a picture on my fridge.

"Aren't they cute?" I said proudly. "That's my sister and her family." I pointed out each of my nephews, smiling.

"Wow, you and your sister sure don't look alike. I'd never know you two were related," Amy said.

"That's because Leslie is my stepsister."

"Oh, I'm sorry! I didn't realize you aren't real family." Amy looked a little embarrassed.

"Oh, but we are 'real' family," I assured her.

I thought back to the stormy days of my early teens when we didn't feel like family at all; then I told Amy the story.

My father left us when I was only two, so for years my "family" was just Mom and me. We were best buddies, spending all our free time together—shopping, hiking, going to movies. I didn't want anything to change.

But when I was about 13, change came anyway. Mom was a feature writer for the local newspaper, and Steve was hired as a sportswriter. Before long she began coming home with stories about brilliant things he'd said. I could tell she liked him.

"You aren't going to date this guy, are you?" I asked.

Mom turned pink. "Well, he hasn't asked me out. But he's a very nice person. He has a little girl too."

"I'll bet he's a monster. That's why his wife divorced him."

"He's a widower. His wife passed away several years ago, and he's had to raise Leslie all by himself. I think he's a wonderful father—I'm sure you'd like him." I saw the dreamy expression on her face and knew I'd lost the battle.

They did go out, of course, and before long we were sharing family activities with Steve and eight-year-old Leslie. She whined about everything—where we planned to go, which movies we watched, what Mom cooked for dinner. I sulked around the apartment, saying as little as possible, hoping Mom would see how miserable I was.

One day I found Leslie in my bedroom, putting one of my new barrettes in her hair. I was furious! I went straight to my mother.

"Can't you see that Leslie looks up to you?" Mom said. "That's why she wants to try on your things. She wants to be just like you."

"She's just trying to take over around here," I retorted angrily. "She thinks everything belongs to her!"

I slammed my bedroom door, but not before I taped a large sign to the outside: "Private! Do Not Enter." Unfortunately, that wasn't the only writing on the wall.

Six months later, Mom and Steve got married. We all moved into a large house on a quiet, tree-lined street. This was a shock for me because I'd lived in an apartment nearly all my life. Although my new bedroom had pretty flowered wallpaper, the house still seemed enormous and unwelcoming and yet, at the same time, crowded. It was crowded with people I didn't consider family, and I was not happy about it.

The first time Mom and Steve decided to go out, they got a 16-year-old neighbor to babysit Leslie—"the rugrat," as I had taken to calling her. They knew better than to ask me to babysit!

I spent most of the evening alone in my bedroom, sulking and feeling sorry for myself. A thunderstorm seemed to be brewing outside, but I paid it no attention. I had the radio turned on loud, tuned in to my favorite station.

Around nine o'clock the babysitter rapped on my door and stuck her head into my room.

"My boyfriend just got here," she announced. "We're going to a party. You'll watch the kid until your parents come back, won't you?" She vanished before I could think of anything to say. I sat on my bed, wondering what—if anything—I should do.

It wasn't until she was gone that I really noticed the thunder—deafening crashes that came one after another and seemed to shake the very foundation of the house. And then I heard something else—crying. I went to investigate.

Leslie was curled up on the twin bed in her room.

"What's the matter?" I asked gruffly.

"I'm scared," Leslie sniffed. "I want Mommy!"

"Mom and Steve will be home soon," I said.

Leslie stopped crying and gave me a wrathful look. "Not *your* mom!" she said coldly. "*My* mom."

I stopped in my tracks when I heard that. At that statement, even my hardened teenage heart softened. Poor kid—at least I knew my mom was coming home tonight, even if I wasn't the only one she came home to anymore.

When Steve and Mom came home, they were amazed to find us together in my bedroom. I'd made some popcorn. The music was blaring, and Leslie and I were dancing with my stuffed animals.

* * *

"I won't pretend that we never fought again or that I never missed having Mom all to myself," I told Amy, "but I started to understand Leslie a little better, and I actually started to think it might be kind of fun to have a sister. And you know what? It was."

Today, I almost can't remember the animosity I once felt. My greatest memories are of times shared with my sister, and I am grateful every day to my mom for bringing us together.

I smiled. "So this is a picture of my sister and her family. Aren't they beautiful?"

Country Comfort

"Oh, I remember this smell," I closed my eyes and breathed in the scent of a cool summer evening rich with memories. I glanced at the small, redheaded woman sitting beside me on a boulder in the middle of a freshly mowed field, sketchpad in hand. She merely smiled, and I knew I'd have to entertain myself until she completed her drawing. My sister, Jenny Lynn, is an artist. Perhaps you've seen her children's books. She specializes in mice, of all things. But not just any mice. Jenny Lynn's mice are almost like people, with histories and families. There are five main characters: three sisters and two brothers. I watched my sister's charcoal dance across the paper. Forty years have passed, but, standing here, my memories are as fresh as the clover underfoot.

* * *

It was the summer of my tenth year.

"The country? All summer?" I cried in disbelief.

My parents nodded. The stricken look on my face was reflected on the faces of my younger sister, Penny, and brothers, Buddy and Jim.

"Your mother needs rest so our new baby won't be born too early. No driving, no chasing around after you kids. Just peace and quiet," my father said. "And you, Lacy, as oldest, need to set a good example so Mother can rest." There was no mistaking what kind of example he meant.

"Who needs another baby," I muttered resentfully. I couldn't believe our parents were making us give up a summer of baseball, swimming at the neighborhood pool, and hanging out with our friends. Instead we were banished to our grandparents' dairy farm.

"Easier to move kids than cows," Grandmother stated, practical as ever. Father was staying home to work two jobs to afford his growing family; Mother was joining us.

After just one week on the farm, cranky, exhausted, and worn out, we decided Father's work must be a piece of cake compared to our chores.

We cleaned milking equipment, carried buckets, hauled feed, changed the animals' water, forked hay for the cows to eat and straw for bedding… after cleaning out old yucky straw. We rebuilt fences, the younger kids holding nails and fetching tools for Grandfather, while I learned to hammer.

"Your mother needs kids strong enough to carry stuff for her after the baby gets here," he said. We flexed our muscles, vying for most improved.

"I need you children to reroute that creek." Grandmother pointed to a muddy spot just beyond her huge vegetable garden. The creek had jumped its banks during spring rains. "Your mother and that baby need fresh vegetables. Can't have the garden wash away."

By midsummer, I was singing a different tune. I had decided that swimming at the pool paled in comparison to the satisfaction I felt after baling hay. Going to the movies with friends didn't hold a candle to riding horseback over hilly meadows to hunt for lost calves and watching Sally the border collie bring "her" calf home safely.

"Just like your Mama's doing with that baby, keeping it from harm," Grandfather said as we unsaddled our horses. Maybe helping that happen was more important than baseball, I admitted to myself, curiosity about the baby nibbling at the edges of my annoyance like a mouse in a feed sack.

"I think you kids are ready for an important job," Grandfather said after supper. "It looks like your baby's going to be needing some things." He showed us some wood. "What do you think—is there something waiting inside this old log to get out?"

A cradle took shape under his skillful carpentry and his even more masterful handling of us, his "young hooligans," as he affectionately called us. The walnut we were using for the cradle came from trees Grandfather's grandparents had planted on this very land.

We loved the aroma as we worked, and we began to imagine the baby in it. Who would she look like? Would she be redheaded, like me? Or blond like the others?

At night we would snuggle close to Mother as she lay on the sofa, resting our heads on her ever-expanding belly and imagining we could hear the baby's pitty-pat heartbeat. This was our introduction to Jenny Lynn. I don't know how, but somehow we all just knew this baby was a girl, a sister, and we began to love her then. No longer simply an inconvenience, she was our sister, unknown but not unloved. We took turns reading to her and Mother throughout those long, hot summer evenings. She assured us Jenny Lynn could hear everything.

"So watch what you say," I cautioned the younger children. "Otherwise, when she's born, she'll scream at the sight of you."

Not long before Jenny Lynn arrived, we finished her cradle. Grandfather even let us carve our names into the bottom.

It's still there, that cradle. It rests by the fireplace in the farmhouse behind Jenny Lynn and me as we sit in the pasture. It's taken on the well-loved, well-used patina of years of service. At family gatherings, we love retelling the story of "growing" our baby sister. Jenny Lynn now lives here at the farm, illustrating her books in the converted barn where the fragrance of hay and cows lingers in memory. Whenever she struggles to finish a picture or can't get it to look on canvas quite the way she sees it in her head, she takes a break and goes into the farmhouse to clear her mind. She stands near the cradle and rocks it gently, evoking soft, soothing thoughts—memories of the family that loved her into being.

*A sister is a gift of God,
sent from above to make
life worthwhile here below.*
—ANONYMOUS

Coming Together

$\mathcal{S}$ometimes, it takes a tragedy to bring people together—even sisters. For years Teresa and Stephanie had lived totally separate lives, sharing only the occasional holiday card or phone call. Although they were in their early 40s, neither had thought to try to establish a real relationship. That is, not until their parents informed them that they planned to divorce after 45 years of marriage. What had seemed like the perfect marriage was completely ripped apart when their father, without warning, left their mother.

Teresa was childless and single, leading the dizzying life of a soap opera actress. Stephanie, on the other hand, was far more traditional, married and settled with a family of her own before she was 30. Their decisions to travel to Kansas City to help their mom through what would be a dark and painful period brought their small con-flicts to a major head.

Each sister came with a plan for Mom. Of course their plans were totally different, as were their responses to their father's decision to divorce. Teresa had a list of men her mother might want to consider as gentleman callers; Stephanie knew of a good therapist and com-munity church. Stephanie internalized her anger toward her father,

not wanting to make any waves. Teresa made quite a few waves before slamming the phone back into its cradle.

Truth be told, both wanted what was best for their mother. And as the days went on, they realized that their constant bickering was getting them nowhere, and they had only created more conflict for their mother. Over coffee late one night, they sat at the kitchen table as their mother slept upstairs, and they talked. First they agreed to listen more to what their mother wanted, and to help her make strides toward those goals. Then they discussed their father, and how both of them had suspected there was something wrong with their parents' marriage. By 3:00 in the morning, they moved on to their own lives.

Both were openly surprised to learn that they often dreamed of walking in each other's shoes. Teresa admitted for the first time in her life that she really did want to marry and have a family. Stephanie laughed as she confessed her envy of Teresa's successful television career. She even admitted to being totally addicted to her sister's soap opera, having rarely missed a show. Teresa laughed so hard she cried when Stephanie reenacted one of her sister's most melodramatic moments, in the end collapsing in a heap on the floor.

The nightly chats became a ritual for the sisters, and their mother started going to bed just a little earlier, with what seemed like a smile on her face. The reality was, they were growing closer and the bond between them grew stronger. As they marched into court with their mom for the final decree, they all held hands and squared their shoulders. A difficult situation was made a whole lot easier for the woman they both loved.

The three of them shed tears when the gavel cracked; they knew they would all mourn for the marriage that no longer existed. That night, all three of them sat up and shared their fears of Mom being alone and financially insecure. But this time, the two sisters rallied behind their mother, directing their love and energy toward her. Stephanie promised her mom that she would never be alone, and Teresa promised her financial security. Each gave from what they had in abundance. Neither realized until their mom hugged them and smiled over her shoulder as she went up the stairs that the real gift they had given their mother, the gift that mattered most, was their newly strengthened relationship.

In childhood, you and your sisters start a relationship that becomes like Grandmother's fine china. When you take it out after years of storage and dust it gently, you'll discover that it's even more beautiful than you remember. And its value has increased immeasurably over the years.

Seven Sisters

It was Thanksgiving day. I was surrounded by loved ones; I was happy. I looked around the room at the large family I had married into. My husband was one of eight children, and the only male. Eight children! Seven girls, one boy. Seven sisters growing up with a single brother in their midst.

I had been plunged into the heart of this big family, struggling to sort out who was who. After we got engaged, half teasing, half serious, my husband sat me down and quizzed me with group pictures, pointing out various sisters and their families and making me memorize names, nicknames, birthdays, and spouse's and children's names. I learned fast.

Seven sisters! I could hardly imagine what life must have been like growing up. Even in a spacious house, there must have been crazy times. Just think of mornings with everyone dashing to get ready for school. Never enough bathrooms, never enough mirrors. It boggled my mind.

Just keeping track of which shoes and clothes belonged to which sister would have been incredibly confusing. I could only imagine

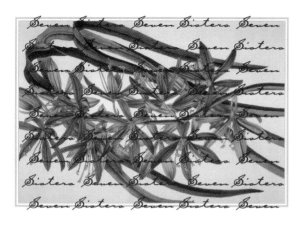

the lack of privacy. And just think of the demand for the telephone line!

By the time I came into the picture, most of the girls were married and out of the house. I studied photo albums and rows of framed pictures, enjoying picking out the familiar faces clustered together in happy scenes. I listened to stories, some funny, some serious, by the hour. I browsed through trophies and keepsakes with my proud mother-in-law, getting better acquainted with my new family.

Yet it never failed to amaze me. Seven sisters. Five older than my husband, two younger. Certainly he had been teased mercilessly and had done plenty of teasing in his turn. Surely there had been squabbles with so many women living together. Surely there had been conflicts.

But what I witnessed over the years were joyous family gatherings, full of laughter, banter, heaps of good food, and fellowship. I watched them enjoying the good times and pulling together through a range of crises, sickness, and worse. Whether to bring casseroles to feed us after the birth of our babies or to loan a car when ours broke down, the sisters were always there, always a solid front to be counted on.

And now, gathered together once more, I thought yet again of how it must have been, all seven sisters growing up together. This time, however, instead of thinking of how wild, how chaotic and competitive it might have been, I thought instead of the incredible gift it must have been. I watched the seven of them inter-act with words, gestures, and looks, and I realized there is nothing in the world that can compare to the bond between sisters. And while one might suspect that the competition and mayhem of seven girls living in one house might have weakened the ties, instead the sisters had united to form a bond no outsider could begin to under-stand. It was as if these women drew their strength from each other, leaning on and supporting each other in whatever ways necessary. Each of them knew immediately what the others needed, and they were quick to provide it without being asked. Watching them, I was almost jealous—except I didn't need to be. Deep though the bond between sisters was, it widened to include their only brother and, by extension, me. I was filled with a rush of love for these seven women whom I had come to call my sisters.

I thought of them marrying, leaving home, moving on with their lives, yet all of them holding tight to the bonds of love and sister-hood that held them together. I studied their faces, thinking how well they meshed together, those seven sisters, how well they joined forces to deal with trouble, how well they stood together to face adversity, and how much they enjoyed spending time in each other's company—each and every one of them—whenever we all got together like this. And how well they had made room for me, the lone sister-in-law among them.

Looking around that crowded room, hearing their happy voices and feeling part of the jostling crowd of family, I shook my head and smiled. It must have been amazing being surrounded by seven sisters growing up. It was amazing enough being surrounded by seven sisters-in-law right now.

There is a double blessing on which the fortunate depend—
it's the joy of having a loving sister who is also a true friend.

Adonis

"Who's that boy you've been looking at?" I asked my 12-year-old daughter as we sat beside a friend's backyard pool.

Jenna flushed. "I'm not exactly looking at him. It's Annie's brother Brad."

"Gee, he's grown since I saw him last. Isn't he about 13 now?"

"Fourteen," my daughter corrected me immediately.

I watched curly-haired Brad stride confidently to the end of the diving board, pause dramatically, and leap into the water with the confidence and abandon seen only in the very young.

I smiled.

"You know, he reminds me of a boy I knew when I was about your age. Your Aunt Linda and I were both in love with him."

"Really? Did you fight over him?"

"Well, let's just say we competed with each other for a while." I smiled as I remembered the events of many years ago. "It all happened around a swimming pool, too. Your grandpa loved to swim, so we were one of the first families in our neighborhood to have our own pool.

"Grandma threw a pool party for Aunt Linda's fourteenth birthday. Linda had a crush on a boy named Jack, but I was starting to notice boys, too, and at the party that day I decided Jack was the most gorgeous guy I'd ever seen.

"Well, we oohed and aahed about him at dinner that night until Grandpa laughed at us. From that time on, he always referred to Jack as 'Adonis.'

"Pretty soon Jack started coming to our house regularly with Linda's friends to swim in the pool. My sister and I would both spend hours fixing our hair, which was ridiculous since we were just going to get wet as soon as we got in the pool! Jack liked baseball, so Linda and I would try to outdo each other by getting Grandpa to teach us who was on which team and trying to memorize stats so we could show off in front of Jack. And Jack flirted with both of us, so we couldn't tell which one he really liked.

"And the more he flirted, the harder Linda and I tried to antagonize each other. I tell you, we were pretty nasty," I shook my head ruefully as I recalled the hard feelings between us.

"Then one day a friend of Jack's told us the truth: Jack didn't want either of us for a girlfriend! He just pretended to be interested in us because he liked using our swimming pool."

Jenna giggled. "Bet you felt pretty silly about fighting with Aunt Linda when you found that out!"

"Oh, we both felt plenty silly. But after we recovered from our disappointment, we decided to play a joke on Jack—and your grandpa helped us.

"He called Jack into our living room for a man-to-man talk. We were hiding in the kitchen, so we could hear the whole thing.

"'Son,' he said, 'I notice you've been paying a lot of attention to my daughters. Now I think it's time you make up your mind which one you're going to marry.'

"I thought Jack was going to have a heart attack! He turned purple and started yelping about how he was only 14 and he didn't even know if his parents would let him date yet.

"'So it will be a long engagement,' Grandpa said. 'Probably a year or two. We believe in early marriages in our family. Meanwhile, you can get ready for your new responsibilities by working for me in the family business after school every day. Of course, I won't pay you anything because you'll be learning—preparing for marriage and a family.'

"Jack took off like a shot! Grandpa didn't even have a chance to tell him it was all a joke. Neither of us saw him for a couple of months. And he never asked to swim in our pool again!

"And once Aunt Linda and I recovered from our broken hearts, we realized something."

"What's that?" Jenna asked eagerly.

"No matter how much we thought we loved Jack, we loved each other more."

Though friends may come and go, a sister is with you forever.

Coming to America

In the 1920s, Ellis Island bustled with European immigrants. Along with her family, eight-year-old Evalina, the youngest of four sisters, left Italy—and all that was familiar—for America. The four girls were only a year apart each, spoke little English, and didn't know what lay ahead of them. The trip across the Atlantic had been awful, especially for Evalina, who was seasick much of the time. Her family couldn't afford the comfortable cabins on the upper decks, so they stayed in the stuffy, musty lower decks of the large ship.

Far above their compartment, ship life included singing and dancing and formal dinners. Evalina and her sisters would sneak off to the stairwells and listen to the grand music. Carmella, the eldest, would dance about, pretending to be a wealthy society woman. Maybe, they whispered, one day they too would dance on the upper deck with handsome men. Carmella imagined a line of men waiting to dance with her while society women whispered about the identity of the beautiful young woman.

The day they finally docked, the four girls stuck together like raisins, holding hands tightly as a mass of immigrants rushed them along. They huddled in fear—and excitement—as their parents stood in line to get their papers stamped. Evalina felt overwhelmed by the people and the noise, but her three older sisters held onto her and she felt heartened.

Carmella watched over her younger sisters as nurses herded them into a medical examining room. Evalina hated the prodding and poking, and the vaccinations were painful. Still, she thanked God they were all acceptably healthy and were allowed to stay in this new country. She and her sisters gathered in yet another corner to wait for their parents to process more papers.

Suddenly, a man grabbed Evalina's hand and tried to drag her away. At first they thought this might be part of the processing; nevertheless, her sisters refused to let go and he could not wrest away all four of them. Their parents, who were in line with several relatives, heard their screams and rushed after them.

Seeing what amounted to an entire squadron of angry family members swarming toward him, Evalina's would-be abductor gave her up without a fight. He even tried to ask for reward money, pretending he had reached the girl first and tried to save her, but thought better of it as the family encircled him, their stares harsh and accusatory. Their parents hugged and kissed the four girls, inspecting them for injuries. Evalina wept tears of relief and gratitude because her sisters had never let go of her. She happily climbed into her uncle's car and breathed a sigh of relief as they drove away from the awful man.

As her three sisters pointed and stared at the passing sights, Evalina was deep in thought. In Italy, her sisters had been her best friends, and now in America, her sisters remained her best friends. This wouldn't be so bad. As long as they had each other, life would be good wherever they lived.

Sisters are like golden links in an unbreakable chain, growing stronger and more brilliant as the years go by.

Read All About It

I had lived as an only child so long that by five years old, I had given up hope of brothers and sisters. This was logical since my mother didn't have a husband anymore and I only had a daddy on weekends. Not that I was unhappy. Mother and I did a lot of fun things, and I had friends over all the time. But at night I used to pretend I had a long-lost sister who would someday bounce into my life, fall at my feet in delight at discovering me, and join me in play.

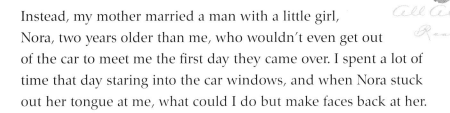

Instead, my mother married a man with a little girl, Nora, two years older than me, who wouldn't even get out of the car to meet me the first day they came over. I spent a lot of time that day staring into the car windows, and when Nora stuck out her tongue at me, what could I do but make faces back at her.

We sat like bumps on a log when forced to be together and, to our credit, didn't act mean, which would have hurt our parents. In that we were instinctively united: protect our parents. We were polite strangers, moving within our own little life circles.

But time, as it does, turns another page, and dreams do come true.

It happened to the sound of tires rolling over pavement seams every Friday afternoon and Sunday night. Thump, thump, thump. Since I divided my time between my parents, we all spent lots of time in the car. And it was there, in the backseat of the old Chevy, that Nora and I first tentatively began building a bridge. "What're you reading?" I asked her one Friday, so bored with coloring books and passing scenery I risked conversation.

She held up *The Story of Jumping Mouse*.

I must have looked wistfully at the "big" words, because, after momentary hesitation, Nora said, "Want me to read to you?"

I nodded. As she read, I edged closer to see the pictures, and when we reached our destination, I insisted we sit in my father's driveway until Nora read the last page. On Sunday's return trip, I pulled a beginning reader from my backpack.

"Will you listen to me read?" I shyly asked.

"Okay."

She had to sit close to help me with the hard words. That night I found several worn books on my bottom bunk bed. "You can borrow them," Nora said, adding severely, "But don't lose them."

I pored over them, *Charlotte's Web*, and young reader versions of *Little Women, Heidi, Treasure Island, Huckleberry Finn*. Sometimes

Nora would lean from the upper bunk to help when I got stuck on an unfamiliar word.

We started packing a sack of books each weekend. "Let's take snacks, too," Nora suggested. We talked about what we were going to read as we slathered peanut butter on bread.

Taking turns, we read aloud, resorting to flashlights as night fell. We had lots of guests with us on those long drives through all those years: Pippi Longstocking, Mary Poppins, *A Christmas Carol's* Tiny Tim and Bob Cratchitt and Mr. Scrooge, Trixie Belden, Nancy Drew, and all the characters from *Wind in the Door*, *Wrinkle in Time*, *The Swiftly Tilting Planet*, and, later, *Wuthering Heights*, *The Swimming Pool*, and *The Tightrope Walker*.

All the mix-and-match grandparents that stepchildren inherit caught on quickly. Nora and I would receive books—sometimes old ones passed on from our parents/stepparents—on birthdays and Christmases. I'll never forget the day Nora discovered that my mother preferred, as she did, Trixie Belden to Nancy Drew. Kindred spirits, they laughed.

By the time Nora and I had outgrown bunk beds and rearranged them into side-by-side twins beneath posters of our favorite music stars and athlete heroines, we had a well-established habit of bedtime reading. We often interrupted our reading to talk about what we'd read.

Last week, Nora sent me the latest Jan Karon book, *A New Song*. It was pre-read, of course, with Nora's tiny notations in the margin, not wanting me to miss some exquisite passage, some simply perfect word.

For more than 30 years, with each page turned, Nora and I have created a relationship that no court could mandate, no parent could force, and no marriage ceremony could guarantee. Quite simply, we're sisters. The truth of our tale is more powerful than the Cinderella fiction of wicked stepsisters. We know how to read around such nonsense and live happily ever after.

Love Letter to My Sister

*D*ear Sarah,

It's six in the morning, and the rain, as it strikes my window, makes the music of a steel drum playing a Caribbean tune: It is happy and melancholy, all at once.

I know what you'd think—me, awake at 6:00 A.M.? I was always the last one out of bed in the morning, famous for wrapping myself in my dreams until hunger drove me from them, while you were the early bird. Well, I guess thoughts of you are what pulled me from my bed this morning.

Remember how Mom was sometimes overwhelmed by the responsibility of raising kids? You always used to say that you couldn't wait to have children of your own, because you were going to be so different. Then I would say, "Not me. I'm not having *any* kids." Yet here I am, planted like an oak tree smack in the middle of the suburbs,

63

surrounded by children. And there you are: as free as the wind and wild as a blackberry bush, growing wherever you choose. You chose not to have children after all. But first you chose to leave us.

It's been 17 years, and still I feel the ache that your absence brings to my heart. I even wrote letters for a while, pretending I could send them to you. I always cried when you didn't write back. I cried because I missed you, but also, I think, I cried for the life that ended too soon.

I know you told me not to cry, but you know what? Crying is what saved me. It broke open my heart and allowed me to feel my grief. It taught me about being human. And about life and death. I think that love is like that: It aches sometimes, a pain that is never quite gone, but like the rain against my window, it becomes the music to which we dance.

And so, dear sister, I am writing to thank you for teaching me about love and life.

So, thank you for getting up with me in the middle of the night when I was afraid—and for telling me funny stories until our laughter rang through the night and drove away the fear.

Thank you for telling me about boys and math and cartwheels. You made growing up seem enchanting and fun.

Thank you for always telling me the truth, even when I asked difficult questions like, "Does everybody die?"

Thank you for all the little things—like giving me your silky pajamas to wear when I was covered with an itchy rash and couldn't bear to have anything rough against my skin.

Thank you, even, for leaving—because you taught me that we define our lives as much by what is missing as by what is present. You also taught me that remaining true to yourself is the only real obligation in life.

Thank you for showing me that love can stretch through time and space to bind two hearts together.

Thank you for keeping my secrets safe in your heart and for allowing me to keep yours; I treasure them.

Thank you for being my big sister. I love you forever…and always.

Love,
Luci

Summer Storm

"It shouldn't take long to clear the place out," Jennie said as she and her twin sister boxed up the colorful Fiestaware dishes. "Fortunately, Mom and Dad always kept the cottage in good shape."

"It needs the cobwebs cleared out, and maybe a new fridge," Josie mused.

I could be talking to the man in the moon, not my twin sister! Josie thought. *Twins separated at birth have more in common than we do.* Nevertheless, she smiled at Jennie as she folded and taped another box.

She surveyed the tongue-and-groove pine walls. Her parents had worked hard to build this place. It had French doors and a window seat that faced the choppy blue waters of Lake Michigan. Through the glass Josie saw her sons, Ryan and Russell, playing with her niece, Alexis. It reminded her of the days when she and Jennie used to run around on the beach themselves.

"These last three years must have been hard," Josie said. "I know Mom and Dad depended on you a lot when they were sick. I really wish I'd lived closer so I could have come home more often."

As Jennie started to answer, a streak of lightning suddenly lit up the sky. It was followed quickly by a thunderclap. The door flew open and Josie's husband, Mark, dashed in, his arms filled with fishing gear. "Rob and I were clearing the shed, but there's a storm coming across the lake. Rob's rounding up the kids, and I brought in some fishing stuff for us to sort through in here."

Just as Rob and the three children rushed in from the deck, the lights flickered and went out. "Mom!" Five-year-old Russell ran to Josie.

"It's OK, honey, we're safe in here." She and Jennie almost ran each other over reaching for candles. The matches were on the mantle, where they'd always been. They lit several candles, melted the ends, and set them on plates around the room.

"There. Isn't that better?" Jennie asked.

"What about our supper, Mom?" Alexis asked. "We can't use the stove. It's electric."

"You're right, but we've got plenty of hot dogs and marshmallows. Daddy can build a fire and we'll roast our dinner over it."

Within 20 minutes the cottage was toasty warm and illuminated by the soft glow of candles and the fireplace. The two families roasted hot dogs and marshmallows as rain drummed on the sloping roof.

Alexis, with her mouth half full, asked, "Did you and Aunt Josie come here when you were little?"

"We sure did. Grandma and Grandpa built this place for us. Aunt Josie and I used to go swimming and canoeing and exploring. We even caught minnows in our sand buckets," Jennie answered.

"You know what we did on rainy days? We played board games and card games. Aunt Jennie and I haven't packed them yet, so I'll bet they're all still in the cupboard."

The three children were soon huddled over a game of Candyland in front of the fire while their parents sat nearby playing cribbage. Both groups were laughing and joking as if they'd spent every vacation of their lives together.

"Are you sure you want to sell this place?" Rob asked as he dealt another hand. "The fishing here is great."

"My grandparents had a cabin in the Allegheny mountains when I was a kid. I could get used to fishing again." Mark tried not to sound wistful.

"The kids would get to know each other if we shared a vacation place," Josie suggested, looking at her sister.

"That's true." Jennie returned her twin's smile.

"Let's take a break out on the deck," Josie suggested. "The rain's starting to let up."

The sisters grabbed their coffee cups and put on the two yellow slickers that hung next to the door. Outside, they stood shoulder to shoulder for a moment and breathed in the smell of the lake and the pine trees. The lapping waves were such a familiar sound that they both sighed and smiled. As always, both started talking at once. They burst out laughing.

"You first, Jo."

"I'm so sorry for not being here for you and Mom and Dad. It was easy to stay away and not face what was happening. But now that

I'm here, I realize that I missed an important part of my own life."
Tears were trickling down Josie's face.

Jennie automatically reached into her pocket and pulled a tissue out
of the slicker. "This slicker must have been Mom's," she laughed.
"She always had a hankie when we needed one!"

Josie blew her nose, then hugged her sister. They stood there in the
cool, clean night air, sharing their first hug in years. Whatever
wounds there had been melted away. The twins found that their
childhood language—no words, just looks—still worked. They
nodded to each other and turned back into the cabin.

"Cousins—families—should stay close," Josie said. "Let's start
unpacking those boxes." The two sisters clinked their coffee cups,
then bumped into each other as they hung up their slickers.

For there is no friend like a sister
In calm or stormy weather;
To cheer one on the tedious way,
To fetch one if one goes astray.

—Christina Rosetti, *By the Sea*

It Runs in the Family

"Don't touch me! Mom, she just hit me!"

"I did not! MOM!"

"She started it!"

"I call front seat!"

"I already called it! You just didn't hear me!"

"STOP IT! MOM! Look what she did!"

"I hate her!"

"She always gets her way!"

"You always give in to her!"

Help! When my daughters go at it like this—and sometimes they go at it incessantly—I lose objectivity and tend to despair: Can't they be nice to each other? Don't they know how lucky they are to have a sister? Sadly, the answer is obvious to me: most of the time, no.

When my second daughter was born, I was so glad she was a girl—not because we could use the clothes outgrown by her three-year-old sister, but because they would have the wonderful experience of being sisters. But it doesn't always seem so wonderful: not for them as they fight; and not for me as I watch, or get called in to arbitrate.

I can't understand it. My own sisters and I get along so well. We not only love each other, but we like and admire each other, too. We all know with absolute certainty that we'll be right there for each other in good times and bad. And we have lots of fun together, and…

"But don't you remember," my mother asks, when I complain to her, "how you fought with your sisters, too?"

Hmmm. If I think really hard I vaguely remember fighting over who got to sit by the window in our '50 Ford; I remember a painting I had to do over about seven times because Andrea kept wrecking it (did I shout "I hate you!"?); I remember Jennifer pushing Andrea out of a tree. I remember envy and tattling, yes, but frankly, it doesn't seem that we were nearly as bad as my daughters are.

"That's because you've forgotten," my mother laughs. "I used to worry that you three wouldn't even speak to each other when you grew up. My sister and I were very close, and unless she reminded me, I always forgot how *we* used to fight. Why, that's how Caroline almost lost half her finger! Because we couldn't agree on who got to cut our baby brother's birthday cake."

Oh, how my sisters and I had reveled in that story, though its gory details never failed to send shivers up and down our spines. But to realize that our own mother—that paragon of maturity and good sense—would have been in a tussle over a knife, just to cut a piece of cake, was marvelous to know. Of course, it was Caroline's fault, Mom always reminded us gravely, because Caroline had grabbed the knife. But my mother—with a marked lack of maturity and good sense—had refused to let go! Whenever we asked our Aunt Caroline about it, she would slowly curl open her hand to reveal the scar, and we would squeal in delighted horror.

What really made it OK, though, was the obvious bond of affection and loyalty my mother and her sister shared. You could just feel how much they liked and loved each other: You saw it in their faces, you heard it in their voices, you felt it in your heart.

My sisters and I have that same kind of bond, and that's what I want for my daughters. Perhaps it just takes some time.

"Monica and I are going to have a farm when we grow up," my 11-year-old, Sophie, tells me as we walk down to the barn one night.

"We'll have 70 acres, and we'll sort of divide it, and I'll live in this part and she'll live in that part, but we'll have trails connecting our houses so our kids can ride the horses or snowmobiles or 4-wheelers back and forth all the time. Our vet clinic will be right in the middle, and I'll be the small animal vet, and she'll be the large animal and emergency vet. I'll make housecalls half the day, while she…"

It amazes me to hear Sophie paint this cozy picture after she was just complaining a few hours ago that her sister tortures her when I send them to the barn together! But suddenly I have enormous hope, because, of course, there *is* a bond here that is deep and strong. I can see it clearly, their future farm with the vet clinic in the middle, and I ask her seriously if they would let me be the receptionist. And I know they'll be good friends when they finally put childhood behind them. And why not? It runs in the family.

"MOM!"

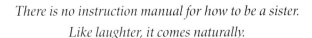

There is no instruction manual for how to be a sister.
Like laughter, it comes naturally.

Forgiveness

I was clumsy as a child and often broke things around the house. But when I accidentally broke my older sister's favorite porcelain doll, I thought my life would be over at the ripe old age of nine.

It was an accident, plain and simple. I bumped into her bookcase, sending the proudly displayed doll crashing to the floor. My mom was outside in the garden, Dad was at work, and Colleen was staying the night at a friend's house, so I did the only thing I could think of. I got the glue and made a measly attempt to glue the doll back together again. I thought my work looked pretty good, but on closer inspection, the cracks and chips were evident. I spent that afternoon and evening alone in my room in a panic, wondering what kind of punishment Colleen would inflict upon me when she got home.

Fortunately, her friend asked her to stay another night! This bought me the time I needed to figure out a way to find the money for a new doll. I checked my piggy bank. Five dollars and loose change, not nearly enough to replace the expensive doll. Try as I might, I couldn't think of a way to come up with enough money. In dread, I waited for Colleen to come home and discover my terrible, unforgivable secret.

The next day I waited in my room, door closed, my knees trembling, listening to my sister come through the front door and walk down the hall to her room. Then there was only silence.

I couldn't take it anymore. I quietly opened my door and peeked down the hall. I saw Colleen standing there, just staring in the direction of the bookcase, and then she turned around. I closed the door and shuddered in fear. What seemed an eternity later, the door opened—and my sister came in and sat beside me. She said she knew that I had broken the doll, and then she was silent. I confessed, tears in my eyes, ready for my punishment. And then Colleen did something I never imagined. She hugged me and told me it was all right, that she knew it must have been an accident, and that there was nothing for me to worry about. She was so nice and sweet, I wondered if she was really my sister. But it *was* her, and I sighed in relief and happiness as she told me I was silly for ever thinking that a doll was more important than a sister.

There are certain things in life on which we can always depend: The sun will come up tomorrow, the grass will grow, and sisters will always, in the end, forgive one another.

The Gossamer Blouse

"**G**randma!" Rebecca bellowed. "Janie's wearing my brand-new jeans!"

"Last week she wore my new tank top, and didn't even ask!" Janie countered. "At least I told her I was going to wear her jeans."

"And I said you couldn't!"

"Girls," I broke in, "that's enough! Now sit down and have some breakfast with me." I patted the table and looked at them.

The girls plopped reluctantly in their chairs, exchanging dark looks.

"Janie," I said, "return Rebecca's jeans." Rebecca stared smugly at Janie. *"This,"* I said emphatically, "is my house rule. No one may borrow anyone's clothing without permission. Period."

The girls glowered at each other, so I threw in an icebreaker. "And that means hands off my new orange muumuu." They looked at each other and rolled their eyes at the mere suggestion they might even consider wearing it. Then they realized I was teasing.

"Oh Grandma, I think your muumuu is safe for now." Rebecca stabbed a waffle from the plate I'd put between them, and threw it on Janie's as a peace offering.

"You know," I told them, "my sister Julia and I once argued over a blouse she bought and I wore first. Let me show you something." I went into the family room and got my oldest photo album.

I opened it and pointed to a studio photograph. "Who do you think that is?"

"Hey—it's you!" Janie said. "Wow, were you pretty!" She looked up at me and added quickly, "Of course, you're *still* pretty."

"Look at that blouse I'm wearing. Isn't it something?" I commented. "It belonged to Julia." The girls looked at the picture, then at me. "Your great-aunt Julia was two years older than me. When she graduated and got a job, she started buying very nice clothes. She and your Uncle Stuart were engaged, and Julia was putting away clothing for her trousseau. I just loved that blouse," I outlined the picture with my finger. "The two of us would take it out of her hope chest just to look at it. We called it her gossamer blouse because it was so light and airy."

"And you asked Aunt Julia if you could borrow it," Janie beamed.

"Well...not exactly. I did ask her, but she said no."

"And you wore it anyway!" They both looked like they'd been stuck with a hat pin.

"The day I had my senior picture taken, I waited for Julia to leave for work, then I 'borrowed' her blouse!"

The girls were dumbstruck. "Did you get into trouble?" Rebecca pumped me for the facts.

"Julia was furious. She said she had planned to wear it for her engagement party, but since I'd worn it first, it wouldn't be special anymore. Then, after screaming that I'd ruined her engagement, she stopped speaking to me."

"So what happened next?" The girls couldn't wait to hear.

"Well, I had been dating a boy named Rob, and suddenly he admitted he'd been seeing another girl. He said he was taking her to the senior dance instead of me. I was devastated! I couldn't sleep, I couldn't eat. All I did was stay in my bedroom and cry." I paused to catch my breath. "It was Julia who snapped me out of it. On the day of the senior dance, she walked into my bedroom carrying the gossamer blouse. 'You're going to the dance,' she announced, 'and you have a date.'

"Stuart's cousin was home on leave from the Navy, and she'd arranged for him to take me. At first I argued, but she was very firm. 'You're going, and you're wearing the blouse.'"

"Did you go?" Rebecca asked.

"I did, and here's the best part. When the doorbell rang, my father answered it, and there stood the most handsome man I'd ever seen! He was tall, with curly black hair and big brown eyes. He was wearing a Navy dress uniform."

"It would be so cool if you'd kept a picture of him," Janie sighed.

"Look here, Ms. Romance." I turned a few pages, and there were my wedding photos.

"It was Grandpa!" the girls squealed.

"We dated for three years. When he finally proposed, I started my own trousseau, but I kept it under lock and key!" I laughed at myself. "We had a beautiful wedding, as you can see." I pushed the album back toward the girls.

 "There's Aunt Julia. Was she your Matron of Honor?"

"Of course she was. And Stuart was the best man."

"What a romantic story!" Janie murmured. "And all because she wore her sister's blouse."

Janie looked askance at her sister. "Maybe I should wear these jeans for a while longer. You never know what could happen."

"Hand them over!" Rebecca demanded.

I sighed loudly and said, "Do you want to hear what happened between your mother and your Aunt Becky?" Both heads spun back at me, eyes wide with anticipation.

"Never mind," I said. "It's not important."

"Oh, yes, it is!"

"If I tell you, will you stop your arguing?"

Janie poured more juice, and the three of us sat back for another shocking story of sibling unrest.

The Marriage of Two Minds

I watched my wife work the crowd. That is one of Amy's most admirable skills—mingling. When she enters a room, every head turns her way. Not because she is drop-dead gorgeous, although I happen to think she is. Not because she sparkles with glamorous jewels or designer clothes: We could never afford such things. But because she exudes charisma.

Fortunately for my wife, yet unfortunately for her sister, Kelly, Amy got a double dose of charm—as if she got her own helping plus her sister's. Fed up with Amy always capturing the spotlight, and unable to cope with the jealousy she felt whenever she and Amy were in the same room, Kelly broke off all communication about five years ago. My wife and her sister had not spoken since then. But now here we all were, at the reception for their cousin's wedding. I watched my wife work the crowd, edging her way toward her sister. I watched Kelly stand tensely in the corner, a habit she exhibited at all family affairs. Dressed in my best blue suit, I wished I was wearing something sturdier, like a bulletproof vest. Verbal missiles were bound to fly. But when Amy reached her sister I saw a softness envelop them both, sweet and light like the inside of a wedding cake. It seemed that time had healed both egos, space had restored sisterly love.

But when I saw my wife point a well-manicured finger at her sister, throw back her head, and laugh, I began to sweat. How rude. This was not my wife's style! Then I saw my sister-in-law follow suit, laughing with even more gusto—if that were possible. I moved closer, curious and more than a little bit wary.

That's when I saw what had brought about their great hilarity. Amy and Kelly were dressed in identical dresses. Not that I'm prone to noticing such things, since my idea of fashion is leaving the house with two matching socks, but I suppose my radar was extra-sharp that afternoon. I heard my wife commend Kelly's good taste. My sister-in-law returned the compliment. From there the conversation entered a rather banal holding pattern, until eventually their topics turned toward the missing five years—what had been accomplished, suffered, enjoyed. I saw Amy touch her sister's shoulder, nodding agreement to some comment; I watched Kelly touch my wife's hair gently. These two sisters, dressed in identical dresses, looked like bridesmaids at their own private wedding. It was the marriage of two hearts, a ceremony celebrating two sisters.

Adopted

"When you were two years old, you were a little monster," Loren announced. She was standing in the doorway of May's bedroom. "Look at this!" She held up the family photo album for May to see, displaying a picture of a tiny girl whose face was covered with white frosting. "This was your birthday party, the week after you came to us."

May had been sprawled across her bed, listlessly painting her toenails and listening to music. Now she sat up and held out her hand for the photo album. The picture made her smile in spite of herself.

"Look at me!" she exclaimed. "What a mess."

Loren sat down on the edge of her sister's bed, and May scooted next to her.

May began turning the pages, absently chewing a fingernail. "Hey, there's Mom and Dad carrying me off the plane."

Loren smiled and rubbed May's shoulder. "Uncle John took that picture. Everybody was so excited about you coming, we didn't sleep at all the night before! It isn't every day you get a new baby sister—especially one who's coming all the way from Korea."

"Exactly what you wanted," May said wryly.

"Well, I *was* a little jealous," Loren admitted. "After all, I was the baby before you got here. It was kind of hard giving up my spot."

May shut the cover on the photo album and crossed her arms. "But I was adopted, so it wasn't the same thing."

"Don't kid yourself. You should have seen the deal the relatives made over you. All that coochie-cooing was absolutely nauseating."

May laughed.

"Remember the sign Tommy, Jeff, and I made?" Loren reached over and opened the book, flipping to another page. There she stood with her two brothers, all three of them looking serious and proudly holding up a lopsided sign that read "Welcome Home, Baby May. We Love You."

Loren turned the page again.

"And here's your first birthday party. Grandma Reynolds sewed you a special dress for the party—and you smeared icing all over it! There were more presents than we knew what to do with—you got tired of opening them about halfway through, so I took over. Here, there's a picture of me ripping through that mountain of gifts!"

May looked closer at the baby version of herself gazing adoringly at her big sister, completely ignoring the new toys and clothes that surrounded them.

"I know I was nuts about you," she said, "but I guess I always felt in the back of my mind that I was an outsider. For a whole year of my life I wasn't part of this family, and then I just showed up. How could you love me—just like that? How could I be your sister all of a sudden?"

Loren lay back against a mound of pillows and stuffed animals. "I guess I felt like any kid with a new sibling. Excited, proud, jealous. I remember the time you were getting so much attention, I packed a grocery bag full of toys and said I was running away from home."

"I guess you changed your mind, since you're still here."

"Yes, I'm still here, even though for a while I felt like you did—that I wasn't part of the family. You were getting so much attention, I thought no one needed me around! But you helped me realize that everybody loved me—even you. You used to toddle around after me everywhere I went. Mom said that was a compliment: It was your way of showing you admired me."

May turned to another page. "Here's our first family portrait." Mom and Dad sat in the middle, and the two boys and Loren were arranged in front of them. Sitting on their mother's lap was two-year-old May.

"Am I holding onto your collar?" May asked, puzzled.

"That's the only way you'd hold still for the picture! You kept saying you wanted to sit on Sissy's lap, but the photographer thought it wouldn't look right because I was so short. So you got hold of me and wouldn't let go. See? I told you you were a little monster back then. That must be what made you so lovable."

"Well, you don't look too upset by it," said May.

"I wasn't upset," Loren said softly. "Not at all."

When My Sister Got Married

*L*ibby was slated to be the maid of honor in her older sister's wedding, and as far as she was concerned, the blessed event could come none too soon. As Rachel had planned and shopped and made arrangements for "her" day, everyone had suffered the pains of tedium that come from too much attention to detail and too little perspective on that detail. Just watching her sister made 16-year-old Libby know that if her time to marry ever came, she would elope.

As W-day grew nearer, Rachel grew more irritable, and Libby couldn't seem to do anything without getting on Rachel's nerves. Since the girls still shared a bedroom, it was a real problem. At one point, Rachel complained that Libby breathed too loudly while doing her homework. "Maybe I could hold my breath for a few hours," Libby snapped. Bad idea. Though practically grown up, Rachel still hadn't mastered the art of rising above the quips of immature siblings. She could still pack a punch. Truly, Rachel was a young bride—she was only 19—and the pressure was getting to her. Still, Libby gritted her teeth, wondering where the "honor" promised in her title was.

Much to everyone's relief, that day in early June finally arrived. It came and went in a hurry—like a whirlwind, filled with swirling images of photographers, tiered and frosted cake, rarely seen family members, handsome groomsmen, flowers, and music. The day scooped Libby up and carried her along and then suddenly deposited her back at home, tired and yet glowing with the magic of her sister's new destiny.

Libby walked sleepily into the room she and Rachel had shared for many years. Libby was not prepared for the wave of emptiness that flooded over her. There in the corner was the place where her sister's record player had been. Over here, the top of Rachel's dresser, where all of her knickknacks and personal items used to reside, was bare. The walls that had been decorated with her artwork were nearly naked now.

Libby had waited for this day. She and Rachel had talked about it and wished for it—wished that they could finally be grown up and have their own space. And now that that day was here, Libby wanted with all of her heart for it to go away, for everything to be back as it had been.

As Libby's eyes clouded with tears over her unforeseen and irretrievable loss, she lay down on her bed and let her sobs of weariness and sadness and confusion come out all together at once. Reaching up to grab for her pillow, her hand landed on a crinkly piece of paper. Libby sat up and sniffled, swiping away tears as best she could. On her pillow was a flat package with a note:

Dear Lib,
I know I've been hard to live with, but I hope you'll miss your big sister anyway. I'm going to miss you. Remember when we used to dance around the room to this? Keep dancing! It makes the time go faster and the day seem brighter.
Love,
Rachel

The package was a Beatles record she and Rachel had nearly worn out with repeated play. Rachel's record player was gone, but there was still one in the family room. Libby managed a trembly smile at the blurry note and gift. She wasn't in the mood right now. And she probably wouldn't feel like dancing tomorrow, either. But Rachel was right, dancing had cheered them up a time or two before. And it was only a matter of time, Libby knew, before she'd be turning up the music to dance again.

I cannot deny that, now I am without your company, I feel not only that I am deprived a very dear sister, but that I have lost half of myself.

—Beatrice D'Este

Character Actors

*W*hen I was in high school, I tried out for the lead role in the school play, *Romeo and Juliet*. So did my big sister, Sally, who was more popular and a lot prettier than me and, it seemed, determined to be better than me at all costs.

The second child, I was tired of living in my older sister's shadow, and I was determined to prove my talent. I spent weeks reading the script and learning the lines, giving it all I had. Unfortunately, for every minute I spent rehearsing, it seemed like Sally spent two.

As we waited out the final weekend before auditions were to take place, we barely spoke. The tension was thick, especially when Sally got a call from a friend who passed on the scoop that Johnny Cassio, the cutest boy in school, was the front-runner for the part of Romeo.

Now it was war. We studiously avoided each other for the rest of the weekend, practicing lines in our rooms so we'd be ready for auditions, each of us determined to be the winner. Intending to spy

on my sister's performance, I snuck down the hall and listened against her closed door. That's when I overheard a telephone conversation between my sister and her friend that made me stop in my tracks. I heard her talking earnestly to whomever was on the other end.

It turns out Sally wasn't quite the monster I had envisioned. She told her friend that she was torn about wanting to be Juliet, because she knew how much the role meant to me. She wanted to try out for the part because she loved her drama class and really thought she might want to be an actress someday, but when she watched me practice she realized I wanted the part more than anything in the world.

"Jessie's my sister," I heard Sally say. "How can I try to take away something that means so much to her?"

I leaned my head against her door for a moment, then quietly walked back to my room. I sat and thought a while, and then I went back down the hall and knocked on her door.

"Sally," I said, "Want to practice some lines together?"

We spent the rest of the day holed up in her room, going over the play, chatting, and laughing. By Monday we were ready for tryouts. We knew our lines and were comfortable in the character. But more than that, we were confident and secure in our roles as sisters.

Your sister might not say "I love you" in so many words, but she shows it in countless ways that you both understand.

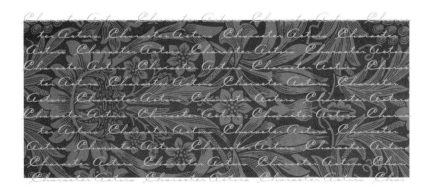

Pettin' Bees

Okay, so I was always jealous of my younger sister Margie. I was tired of hearing about what a good baby she was, especially when I was always being told, "Diana, don't!" And I was tired of hearing about how she was just so darn cute, and was just my dad all over again. Actually, she was a little cutie, so cute you just wanted to pinch those Gerber-baby cheeks, and I'm afraid I did, a bit too hard, more than once.

Oh, she acted innocent enough, with those soft dark ringlets and wide brown eyes, but within those eyes (perfectly framed with their long black lashes), I thought I could detect more than a hint of smug satisfaction.

So, one day, feigning friendship, I grabbed hold of Margie's chubby little hand and took her toddling out into the backyard to find some fun. I was about four years old, and the little princess was about 18 months. She followed along, gurgling happily.

Me: Oh LOOK at the cute little furry bee!

Her: Da-da!

Me: Yes, it IS soft and friendly!

Her: Ga-ga!

Me: Sure, go ahead and pet it. Bees LIKE to be petted!

Yes, she got stung, and yes, I got punished.

Remember, though, I was only a little kid myself when I suggested she pet the bee, and the only excuse I could offer then was that she was just too darn cute—not to mention good—for my liking. But as I grew, my reasons for such actions became much more justifiable: self-defense. As any older sister or brother will confirm, we simply cannot abide having younger siblings hang around spying on us all the time.

It seems unfair to me, even now, that people gasp when my sister tells them about the time I locked her out on our great-aunt's tin roof with the bats. Okay, well, maybe it does sound horrible. But what actually happened was this: My cousin Sally and I were talking older-girl talk (we were probably about nine), and Margie, as usual,

was hanging around trying to listen. When we told her to scram, she pretended to leave but really just went around the corner and lurked behind the door, trying to overhear the highly important and confidential stuff we were saying. So, just trying to find some privacy, we climbed through the window out onto the roof. Surely, since she was only about six, she would not try to follow. But she did. So we got the bright idea to sneak back inside and shut the window.

Strangely, our parents didn't see it as quite the good idea we did, and yes, we were punished.

It seemed like whenever my sister got hurt, even innocently, I got blamed. I'll never forget how we used to play circus, and our favorite part was "fly through the air." I, being bigger than Margie, would lie on my back and lift her up into the air with my legs, where she would hover, arms and legs extended like Superman, giggling uncontrollably. She always begged to play it, and usually it went well, but sometimes my legs gave out, or she flew into the wall or the headboard of the bed. Whoops! Those really were accidents. They were!

Of course, I didn't always torture my sister. There were times when we'd snuggle together under a sheet on a summer night, and since she was scared of the dark, I'd say, "Okay, let's talk about Christmas!" That always got her to forget her fears and begin making wishes. Or we'd be spending a few weeks with an aunt, and except for maybe telling her there was a tiger in the basement, I was pretty nice.

All that sibling torture … Was it really worth it? Only to HER, I'm afraid—she still gets a lot of mileage out of the bee story, even more than the one about getting locked out on my aunt's roof.

But while they may forgive us, you can be sure they'll never forget. On a recent birthday, my sister sent me a lovely card with two little girls holding hands, skipping through a meadow full of bright flowers. On the inside she had written, *"Bzz-zzz."*

No, she'll never let me live it down. But, fortunately for me, in addition to all her other good qualities, she also has a great sense of humor.

Checkers

As young girls sharing a bedroom, my sister, Jordan, and I developed a favorite bedtime routine: a game of checkers. We had received an inexpensive set for Christmas one year, and for some reason we both really took to the game. Even before we could read well enough to understand the instructions, Jordan and I hopped the red and black disks around the board, pretending we knew what we were doing and enjoying every minute of it. Sometimes the playing pieces were red dragons and black monsters or red snakes and black frogs. Other times we'd just make interesting geometric patterns out of the pieces.

This shared ritual became a way for us to wind down after an exciting day. As we grew up and moved into separate bedrooms, we began meeting in the living room or at the kitchen table for our nightly bout of checkers. Sometimes it was all business—a serious one-on-one—and hotly competitive. But more often, it was merely a way to relax—and the means for bringing us together to laugh and talk.

The busier we were and the more stressful our lives became, the more we relied on our checker games to help us relax and spend time together. Over time, our schedules became more varied and our night-time hours filled up with various tasks and responsibilities. Between studies, jobs, and social lives, we were seldom home at the same time. Then sharing a game of check-ers became a rare treat.

That was years ago. Now we live on opposite coasts, and checkers is only a fond memory. Both of us have families and careers of our own. Despite our attempts to keep in touch, phone calls are cut short in order to resolve the latest family crisis or to get the kids to soccer practice.

Recently, a business conference brought Jordan to my city for a rare visit. Her meetings and appointments took most of the day, but she planned to come to my house as soon as she could get away that evening. As she stepped out of the taxi, I thought how great she looked in her expensive-looking power suit. I thought how smooth and confident she appeared—so different from the tousled-haired girl I'd known.

After the initial excited greetings and hugs, we brought her carry-on bag and briefcase into the house and got settled. Then, I told her of the special surprise I had planned in honor of her visit: dinner reservations at the most popular restaurant in town.

"Thanks, but no thanks," Jordan said flatly. I was bewildered, but a familiar smile crept across her face. "There's only one thing I need right now."

With that, she kicked off her high heels, unbuttoned her double-breasted jacket, hiked up her skirt, and plunked down on the carpet in the family room.

"Grab the checkers, sis," said Jordan. "I'll even let you be the red dragons this time."

A sister knows your true shoe size, your dress size, and hair color, but, most important, she knows the things that touch your heart.

Picking Up the Pieces

I arrived at the airport an hour early. I needed the time to add the finishing stitches on the quilt I've been working on for thirty years. You'd think a quilt could be finished in less time than that, but, as I've always said about quilts, they have a story to tell if we will only let them. This one, a lovely patchwork tale, began its first chapter with two little girls curled at the foot of their mama's bed like kittens in a puddle of sunshine. She would read to us, story after magical story, this gentle, frail woman who loved violets and lily of the valley. The nightgown she wore that last spring was of sprays of spring flowers. After she died, I snuck it into my room and hid it inside the leg of my snowpants. Nobody missed it or Mama's favorite red-checked tablecloth because there was much to tend to in those days. My little sister, Merilee, and I were what needed the most tending, but our daddy just wasn't able. He was working three jobs to pay off Mama's medical bills and was never home. The state lady said we either had to find some better way or we would become "foster," whatever that was. I listened at the door while she talked to my daddy.

And that's how Merilee got taken away from Daddy and me. Merilee was the prettiest little thing. All blond and smiley, a slip of a girl, who always needed my help with zippers and buttons. She was crying the day the state took her away, with everything she owned tied up in a paper bag. But I have to confess she didn't have all her clothes in that bag—I'd taken a blue dress she loved even though it was too little and a pink pinafore that made her look like a doll.

It wasn't long before I followed Merilee into "foster," but we weren't together. Nobody would say where she was. I slept with Mama's nightgown wrapped around my pillow like a pillowcase, and I cut Merilee's dress into handkerchiefs. One of the foster ladies made quilts, and she's the one who looked at my "handkerchiefs" and said, "Why now, Jessica, those look just like quilt squares."

So I cut up more from Merilee's dress and some from Mama's gown and tablecloth. Before I knew it, I had a big square of little squares sewed together. "A doll quilt," the foster lady said. It wasn't, though; it was the beginning of the quilt I'm working on this very minute. I like to think of it as the heart of the quilt.

This foster lady gave me some of her squares, and they're the next section of quilt; they tell of the comfort I found in her home and of the hope she gave me, for she told me if I tried real hard, someday I would find my sister.

Those pieces are framed by scraps from a Brownie uniform someone gave me so I would fit in with the other kids; there are also bits of a Christmas dress from that same period of happiness. Mixed in is the wool plaid of school uniform skirts from the time when the next foster family sent me to school with their children. That's when I decided I wanted to do well in school so I could someday get a good job and make enough money to find Merilee.

Row upon row, my squares radiated out from that central spring-flower of Mama's nightgown, adding color and texture as I put together my life. School, college, marriage—I love to feel the satin from my wedding dress and the stubbly weave from my husband's suit—and then nursing school, the hospital job. The crisp white squares of my first uniform fill in between the pretty patterns of maternity clothes I wore when I was carrying our babies.

My children have asked me since they were old enough to talk, "Who are you making that quilt for?"

And I would explain, as I've had to do today to the interested folks here at the airport, that I was quilting my little sister the life she'd missed sharing. As I quilted, I was hunting. I wrote letters, made phone calls, took trips, embarked on many wild goose chases. And then, finally, one day—I wore the paisley blouse that day, its sheen bright beneath my fingers now—I found Merilee. I'm adding that square now, but I'm leaving the quilt unfinished so we can add something from today.

I hope she likes the quilt. I haven't told her about it, just about how much I've thought about her each day since we were separated. How I kept her with me by telling her a story each night before I went to sleep.

As I wait in anticipation for Merilee's flight to be announced, I look at the quilt, this work of love and hope. Life is a collection of moments tossed into the air, I realize. They land, rearranged, in a mosaic of time as hues of yesterday and today come together in a counterpane of love.

Growing up, sisters weave a unique bond that ties them
to each other with silken skeins of love, laughter,
and memories.

Don't Cry

I tried to be quiet. Mom worked hard all day, and I didn't want to bother her. But I guess I cried louder than I realized. I felt so miserable, I almost didn't care how loud I was. I pushed my face into my pillow, pulled the afghan over my head, and sobbed, hard. All I

could think about were the awful, hateful words I'd heard at school. A bunch of kids had made fun of me, talking about how dumb I looked, what a loser I was, how I never did anything right. It took all my strength not to run right out the door sobbing in front of them. Somehow I held on until dark, when I could sob alone in my room. I'd never felt so terrible before in my whole life. I felt ugly and stupid, like nobody liked me at all and never would. I was worthless. Everything they had said felt true.

I barely noticed when somebody walked quietly into my room. At first I thought it was Mom. I didn't look up. I felt a hand cautiously patting my shoulder, pulling away the comforter I had yanked over my head, and wiping at my eyes with a tissue. I looked up into my little sister Gillian's face. She wasn't so little anymore, almost a teenager, too.

"Shh," she whispered, soaking up my tears, patting me as if she were the older sister instead of me. "Don't cry, Hillary. It's all right."

I sobbed harder. I couldn't help it! I felt so awful. Nobody liked me, I was no good, nobody would ever love me. I'd be alone all my life.

"Hillary," Gillian whispered close to my ear. "Don't cry. Don't feel bad. You're the prettiest, smartest, nicest, best sister in the whole world," she told me. "When I grow up, I want to be just like you. There's nobody as nice as you are."

I stared at her through hot, swollen eyes. Her face looked so serious, so grown up. She meant every word. I could tell. And suddenly, I believed her. She reminded me about some of the nice things I'd done for her that I'd forgotten. She told me she believed in me. And I knew it was true. I felt better, a lot better, knowing I mattered to somebody.

The kids at school never made me cry again after that. Their meanness never touched me that deeply again. My sister believed in me. Her faith in me kept me going until eventually I believed in myself, too.

A sister is a friend who listens with her heart.

Teensy~Weensy

"Thank you," I told the mail carrier, after signing for the small package. A smile tried valiantly to free itself as I shook the package. It gave a satisfying rattle.

I knew what it contained, and my gloom immediately began to lift. Holidays are difficult when you live alone, as I was finding out for the first time. It had been barely six months since my Arnold had passed, but leave it to a sister to brighten even loss's darkest corners. Carrie has been doing that as long as I can remember.

It had been a dark November a half-century ago. Coal dust covered our town, just as fear did our lives.

In the early '50s, our Southern town lived under the shadow of "The Bomb." We were close to Oak Ridge, Tennessee, with its strategic location, and this was predicted to be "the" year when bombs might fall. At school, where I was in third grade and Carrie in fifth, fire drills were replaced with air-raid drills, and room mothers drove their cars to practice taking children on evacuation routes. Carrie and I had already conceived a brave plan to escape and go home. Our family would stick together, we vowed, even concocting a plan to get our father home from work so he could hide in the basement with the two of us, five-year-old Judith, our baby brother Sean, and Mother.

How big a celebration can you plan to ring in the holidays under such a threatening cloud?

Since Halloween, our family had worried the question like a dog with a bone but found no easy answer. Finally, our parents opted for streamlining our holidays in case we had to make a quick evacuation. It took Carrie about a minute to translate the word "streamlined" into: *No Christmas tree.*

No tree? Unthinkable.

Not to worry, Carrie said.

I knew she was up to something when the old cigar box she'd painted and decorated with gold rick-rack, buttons, and jewels she swore were real was gone from the dresser we shared. She kept her treasures in it along with her hoarded tooth-fairy money, leaf-raking coins, and her twelfth-birthday silver dollar.

Smiling in triumph, she unveiled her secret that night at supper. It was the smallest tree I had ever seen: a small gold lapel pin in the shape of a Christmas tree. We children took turns wearing it right

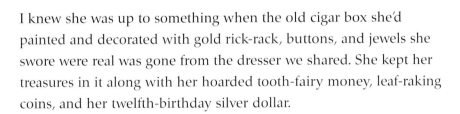

next to our hearts when it wasn't propped in a flower pot on a nest of fake snow. True, its surroundings dwarfed it, but as Carrie pointed out, when you squinted, it looked larger. And it was big enough.

Carrie's determination was contagious. In a moment of high-spirited defiance, Mother ordered a turkey from the poultry man, and Father resumed his hammering in the garage that doubled as his workshop.

Christmas morning arrived in a flurry of snowy grace. There was, at least for the moment, peace on earth. Our presents surrounded the splendid tiny tree in its flower pot nest, shining far brighter than anything that small had any right to do, as my Mother said in bemusement. Carrie's funny little tree changed what could have been a bleak holiday into one that continues to dazzle even in memory.

Over the years, Carrie has sent the pin, with a strict admonishment to return it to her promptly after the holidays, to any family member who needs some extra holiday spirit. Each time, spirits lift, bruised feelings brush themselves off, and hope brings possibilities into life-size proportion.

It's going to be a wonderful Christmas after all.

Wanted: Sister

IMMEDIATE OPENING: Looking for team player committed to exceptional standards and service. Ideal candidate will have ability to analyze situations and adopt an effective, reasonable course of action under stressful situations, and will embody the qualities of honesty, integrity, and accountability. You will enjoy enormous amounts of laughter, conversation, and affection. Secrets will be kept in strict confidence. Unconditional love will be given without regard to past mistakes. *Only individuals capable of making a long-term commitment will be considered for this highly rewarding position.*

Applicants should have the following qualifications:

❧ Good listening skills (psychology degree helpful but not required; immediate on-the-job training will be provided for the right individual)

🙚 Faculty for speaking own mind (as well as ability to bite tongue when appropriate)

🙚 Shoulders soft enough to cry on and strong enough to share the challenges of a lifetime

🙚 Friendly telephone voice—must *enjoy* talking on the phone and be willing to answer calls at any time of day or night

🙚 Access to Internet (especially e-mail) helpful but not required

🙚 Great sense of humor

🙚 Ability to dance like no one is watching

Position also requires tolerance, selective recall, and knack for forgiveness. Finesse in social situations will be rewarded in kind. Willingness to cover refrigerator with pictures of nieces and nephews will be appreciated, and unwavering loyalty is an absolute requirement—*tests will be administered!*

Enjoy outstanding benefits and unlimited opportunity for advancement. We offer a comfortable work environment and flexible shifts—work full- or part-time at your convenience. No dress code has been established (however, we prefer that you wear the same size clothes and shoes, for swapping purposes). Free child care is available on-site, as well as parking and coffee or tea. Recipes may be exchanged freely. Unlimited counseling provided at no charge.

We offer a generous retirement plan: All contributions will be matched, regardless of size or type. Supportive team management and continuous training will be at your disposal.

Looking for respect and support? This may be the opportunity you've been waiting for! Come join the family and have fun while you learn. Successful candidate will have a secure position for life.

Apply in person.

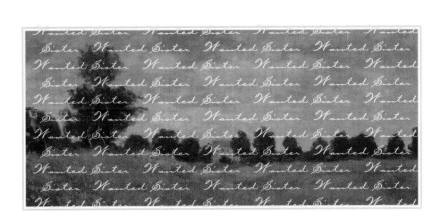

That's My Sister

Megan could hardly sit still. That was her little sister up there on the stage! Megan thought she'd pop, she felt so excited. Her sister was the valedictorian of her class—a tremendous achievement. The smile Megan felt spreading across her face couldn't be stopped.

"That's my sister," she told the woman sitting behind her, who nodded and smiled politely. But Megan couldn't stop there. "My little sister. She's really something, isn't she?" Her parents, sitting on either side of her, smiled indulgently.

As the awards program continued, Megan twisted and turned in her seat, whispering to anyone near enough to listen. "That's my sister. This is so great!"

Megan grinned and grinned until her face ached. It didn't matter that she'd never missed a chance to torment her younger sister as they were growing up. Constant teasing was part of being an older sister, one of the perks. Over the years she had played practical jokes on Courtney, called her annoying nicknames like "Little Bit," even managed to get her in trouble with Mom and Dad once in a while, telling on her whenever an opportunity came up.

And of course she gloated over all the firsts—being first to get her ears pierced, first to wear makeup, first to be allowed to date, first to get a driver's license. A lot of the enjoyment of getting to do all those things was doing them before her younger sister did. But that was part of being the older of the two. It was part of her responsibility as big sister to do everything first. Well, except for being valedictorian. Her grades had never been as good as Courtney's.

Megan jiggled in her seat, almost too excited to sit still. Sure, sometimes it seemed like she and Courtney spent more time arguing and bickering than anything else. But it didn't really mean anything. They were sisters.

When the awards program ended, everyone headed for the reception area, heaping their plates with snacks. Megan skipped the refreshments. She felt too keyed up to eat. She wandered around, watching for familiar faces. Every time she spotted somebody she

knew, she rushed up to tell them about Courtney's award, as if they hadn't all been sitting right there.

"That was my sister up there," she told everybody she saw. "Isn't this great?"

No matter how many times she said it, Megan couldn't quite express how happy she was. No one seemed to understand the depth of her pride.

Grinning and bragging, Megan roamed the room, having a wonderful time, then suddenly she bumped right into her sister.

Hugging each other tight, the two sisters laughed together. Courtney had caught Megan in the act.

"You're embarrassing me," Courtney protested.

Megan smiled and squeezed Courtney tight, letting the hug speak more eloquently than she ever could.

Little sisters follow you constantly, imitate your every move, and are forever getting into all your things, including your heart.

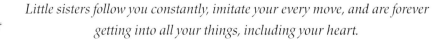

Worth the Wait

$\mathcal{I}$t all began with a phone call. I was busy washing clothes in preparation for my return to college.

"Hello?" I answered impatiently, assuming it was someone for my mother and eager to get back to my chores.

"Melanie?"

"Yes," I replied to the unknown voice.

"This is Janet. How are you?"

I knew about Janet. She and I had lived together when I was very young. She was much older than I, and we never really knew each other the way most sisters do. I had often wondered about her, thought about her, and imagined at times that she and I were friends. But circumstances had made it impossible that such thoughts would ever become reality, and I had grown up an only child, despite the fact that I had a sister who lived not far from me.

"I…I'm OK. Why are you calling?" My suspicious nature came through, and I was anxious to know the bottom line: What did she want?

117

"Well, I wanted you to know that Dad is sick. I thought you might want to come see him."

Dad. What a strange word to me. Ever since my parents had divorced when I was four, the word "dad" meant nothing to me. Neither did "sister," really. And now I was faced with both.

"Well, I guess I do. I haven't seen him for 16 years, you know. Are you sure he wants to see me?" *After all,* I thought, *he was the one who left me.* Where had he been all these years? Where had *she* been, for that matter? The divorce had separated more people than just my parents.

"Yes, he asked for you," Janet replied. "We both want to see you. Can you come?"

"I'm leaving for school later today," I answered a little coldly. "Exactly where would I be going?" I didn't even know where this part of my family lived. How strange to hear a voice that shares your heritage and not be able to picture the face.

"We live just 15 miles from the university. I could meet you there tomorrow and bring you back to the house for a visit. What do you think?"

I felt confused, a mixture of both happiness and fear at the same time. What would my mother say? She hated the man who had fathered me. She had never wanted me to have anything to do with him, or with Janet, who had chosen to live with him instead of with her own mother. What should I do? This might be my last chance to know them. If I was ever going to have a sister, I would have to go now.

"I'll meet you by the big clock at ten tomorrow," I said.

It was settled. I would soon meet my father and sister.

The next morning, I waited anxiously, not quite knowing what to expect. Was I doing the right thing? Would I be creating a new family rift with my mother? Or was this an opportunity for me to finally break free from the anger and burdens of the past and move forward with my life?

I saw Janet walking slowly toward me. She was beautiful, with long black hair, big blue eyes, and a smile that instantly made me feel loved and wanted. We stood staring at each other, trying to detect our common features, wanting to hug but waiting to see what the other would do.

We walked toward her car, a Volkswagen convertible.

"I like your car," I said, admiring its bright red color.

"Thanks," she replied. "I like Bugs."

"So do I—mine is white." We laughed at our similar taste in cars and soon discovered we had other things in common as well—we both loved music, chocolate, and old movies. The potentially difficult drive to see my father was cushioned by the softness of my sister's voice. She embraced me without even touching.

He walked to the door slowly, waiting for me to enter his house. *This frail man is my father*, I thought. We barely spoke, neither of us knowing what to say and each worrying that we'd say something wrong. Janet made us some lunch—soup for him and sandwiches for the two of us.

"Melanie is going to be a schoolteacher, Dad. She's in her third year of college. Isn't that great?"

"Yes," he said. "I'm very proud of you. Your sister wanted to go to college, but I never had the money."

"That's OK, Dad," Janet said, patting his hand. "I have a great job at the bank." Her compassion and love for him surprised me. All I'd ever heard from my mother was that he was a bitter, angry man. I had believed her, and I had assumed Janet would be the same way. I was wrong.

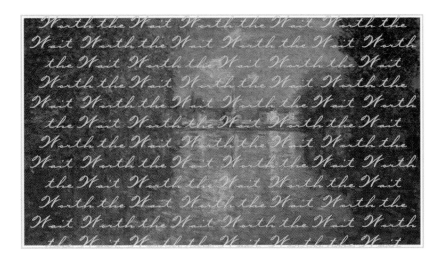

The visit was short because my father's health was declining so rapidly. I hugged him good-bye before I left, and Janet drove me back to my dorm. She thanked me for coming and handed me a package. "Here are some pictures and other things I thought you might like to have. You can keep what you want and give the rest back to me. I'll call you in a few days."

The package contained images of a world unknown to me. But it was a world I was a part of. There were photos of Janet being crowned homecoming queen, my dad catching a huge fish, my family at play. Then there was an old black-and-white photo of a young girl holding a baby. Both girls were smiling. On the back, someone had written, "Melanie and Janet." My heart sank as I thought of all the times I had longed for a sister, a friend, a soul mate. We had missed out on many years together, our lives divided by hurt and anger and fear. But now my sister had returned, reaching out and holding me once again. I knew I had to let go of all the pain and bitterness and forgive my parents for keeping us sisters apart. We had been given a chance to reconnect, and I wasn't about to pass up the opportunity.

Janet and I attended our father's funeral together. We buried him and mourned his passing, but in the midst of the sadness, we found a cause for celebration: Our father's death had brought us back together again.

I regret that I've lost so many years with my sister, but I thank God every day for bringing Janet back into my life. She was well worth the wait.

The relationship between sisters is like a perennial garden—beautiful things sprout untended, often when you least expect it.

My Hat Looks Good on You

*W*hen my younger sister and I were growing up, I always took the lead. I showed her how to dress her dolls, I helped her learn the difference between a lowercase "b" and "d," I told her when it was time to stop wearing socks with her sandals. I must admit, I was the one who even taught her to apply lipstick after she got to school—a good six months before Mom permitted makeup. But on the day I delivered my first child, there were actually two relationships born...my relationship with my new child as well as a new connection between two sisters.

You see, my younger sister already had two children. She'd been there, done that, and lived to happily tell the tale. I, on the other hand, was a rookie at this motherhood stuff and was amazed to find that the entire concept scared the hospital gown right off me. But

without missing a beat—or a labor pain— my sister stood by my hospital bed for the entire grueling 18-hour delivery process. First she gently coached me, encouraging me to breathe. It seems I had forgotten the ins and outs of that simple task! I heard her words, I tried to inhale and exhale, but when the pains struck I began this odd puffing and wheezing procedure, which my sister quickly recognized as confused attempts at Lamaze.

"Forget what you learned in class." my sister suggested. "Just follow me. Don't think…for once in your life, don't think. Just follow."

And so I did. By the end of the first hour, she had me in a pattern. Behind her, though, she heard a counterbeat, a repetitive clunking noise. It was the sound of a waiting father-to-be as he paced the delivery room floor. So next my sister coached my husband.

"Gene," my sister instructed, "Take my place. Stand here, and relax. Everything's okay. This is a wonderfully normal labor. *Normal*. Breathe. Talk about the color you want to paint the living room."

Even in the throes of a contraction I managed to grin. My sister knew that repainting the living room topped my to-do list. She also knew that in my present condition, I could get my husband to agree to absolutely anything I wanted. So when the pain subsided, conversation turned to alabaster white ceilings, mint walls, and sage trim. I even got my husband to agree to new window treatments, or at least that's what I told him three months later—when the redecoration project became reality.

All afternoon and well into the evening, my sister produced cup after cup of ice chips, lollipops for me as well as my nurses, a band to hold back my tousled, sweaty hair. I never once asked for any of these welcome favors: They simply appeared, and I accepted my sister's new role as the leader. As my little sister guided my husband and me toward parenthood, she never once pulled rank on me or flaunted her new position of command. Instead she most gracefully wore my old hat as leader. I gratefully surrendered to her instructions, following her lead and her word until finally, hours later, I held my beautiful new daughter in my tired arms.

My relationship with my sister was never the same after my daughter came into this world. It was better. I had finally learned that we were two adults, each of whom brought something tremendous to the table reserved for family.

To say a friend is "like a sister" is to pay the ultimate compliment.